CHRIST'S SECOND COMING

Thomas Ice and Timothy Demy

HARVEST HOUSE

Scripture quotations are taken from the New American Standard Bible, © 1960, 1962, 1963, 1968, 1971, 1972, 1973, 1975, 1977 by The Lockman Foundation. Used by permission.

Cover design by Left Coast Design, Portland, Oregon.

All views expressed are solely the individual authors' and do not reflect the position of any governmental agency or department.

THE TRUTH ABOUT CHRIST'S SECOND COMING

Copyright © 1998 by Pre-Trib Research Center
Published by Harvest House Publishers
Eugene, Oregon 97402

ISBN 1-56507-848-9

ortion of this book may be reproduced in any form without
Publisher.

Contents

Introduction: 7

---PART 1---

What Is the Second Coming?

1. Where does the Bible teach about the second coming? **8**

2. What is the relationship between Christ's first and second coming? **11**

3. Is the second coming physical or spiritual? **12**

4. What biblical terms are used to refer to the second coming? **12**

---PART 2---

What Is the Purpose of the Second Coming?

5. Why is the second coming necessary? **14**

6. How does Israel relate to the second coming? **15**

7. How do the nations relate to the second coming? **16**

8. How does the church relate to the second coming? **17**

9. How does creation relate to the second coming? **18**

10. How do sin and Satan relate to the second coming? **18**

11. What are the major events surrounding the second coming? **19**

12. Where will the second coming occur? **20**

---PART 3---

When Will the Second Coming Occur?

13. *Are the rapture and the second coming simultaneous?* **21**

14. *Why are the rapture and the second coming separate events?* **21**

15. *Why is an interval necessary between the rapture and the second coming?* **25**

16. *Are there signs for the second coming?* **28**

17. *Has the second coming already occurred?* **28**

18. *What is the relation between Armageddon and the second coming?* **28**

---PART 4---

What Will Happen After the Second Coming?

19. *Why does the millennium follow the second coming?* **29**

20. *What judgments occur at the second coming?* **31**

21. *Why is there a 75-day interval between the second coming and the millennium?* **32**

22. *What will Jesus do after the second coming?* **34**

23. *Is the second coming Christ's final return?* **35**

---PART 5---

Why Does the Second Coming Matter?

24. *Why should I be concerned about the second coming?* **35**

25. *How should people prepare for the second coming?* **36**

Conclusion **39**

Recommended Reading **39**

Notes **42**

About this series...

The Pocket Prophecy series is designed to provide readers with a brief summary of individual topics and issues in Bible prophecy. For quick reference and ease in studying, the works are written in a question-and-answer format. The questions follow a logical progression so that people who read straight through will receive a greater appreciation for the topic and the issues involved. Each issue is fully documented and contains a bibliography of recommended reading for those people who desire to pursue their study in greater depth.

The theological perspective presented throughout the series is that of premillennialism and pretribulationism. We recognize that this is not the only position embraced by evangelical Christians, but we believe that it is the most widely held and prominent perspective. It is also our conviction that premillennialism and, specifically, pretribulationism, best explains the prophetic plan of God as revealed in the Bible.

The study of prophecy and its puzzling pieces is an endeavor that is detailed and complex—but not beyond comprehension or resolution. It is open to error, misinterpretation, and confusion. Such possibilities should not, however, cause any Christian to shy away from either the study of prophecy or engagement in honest and helpful discussions about it. The goal of this series is to provide all those who desire to better understand the Scriptures with a concise and consistent tool. If you will do the digging, the rewards will be great and the satisfaction will remain with you as you grow in your knowledge and love of our Lord Jesus Christ and His Word.

INTRODUCTION

"He will come again to judge the living and the dead." Throughout the centuries faithful Christians have pronounced these words and proclaimed this truth in a score of creeds of Christian orthodoxy, including the Apostles' Creed. Belief in the physical return of Jesus Christ to the Earth is the historic and biblical position of Christianity. Its acceptance is biblical affirmation; its denial is doctrinal aberration.

A recent poll by *U.S. News & World Report* found that a majority of Americans believe Jesus Christ will return:

> Belief in apocalyptic prophecies is not just a phenomenon of the religious fringe. According to a recent U.S. News poll, 66 percent of Americans, including a third of those who say they never attend church, say they believe that Jesus Christ will return to Earth someday—an increase from the 61 percent who expressed belief in the Second Coming three years ago.[1]

But what do we know about the coming of Christ? Is it only a heartfelt hope and historical hype? Or do we have a clear and certain word from God on the second coming? Though many people may not realize its significance, the return of Jesus Christ to Earth is the most important event that will occur in the future.

Grocery store tabloids routinely carry outlandish and exaggerated "prophetic" scoops of Christ's return that have nothing to do with biblical truth. Only in the Bible do we find the definitive source for knowledge of God's prophetic plan. The second coming of Jesus Christ is as certain as the historicity of His first coming. The Bible is not silent on events surrounding the return of Jesus Christ. We know a great deal about His return, and through careful study of God's Word we can gain an understanding of the future that will affect the way we live our lives in the present.

The future is not all gloom and doom. Although it holds trials of an unprecedented nature in human history, it also contains the glorious return of Jesus Christ to establish His righteous reign in preparation for the eternal state. The history of the Old Testament era was one of expectation for the first coming of the Messiah. The history of the New Testament (and our own era) is one of expectation for the second coming of the Messiah. Such an expectation is voiced when we pray, "Thy kingdom come. Thy will be done."

8   *The Truth About Christ's Second Coming*

Christ's kingdom will come when He returns and all of creation will acknowledge Him, the hope of history. Let's see what the Bible says about that coming!

PART 1

What Is the Second Coming?

1. Where does the Bible teach about the second coming?

Prophecy permeates the pages of Scripture. "The number of prophecies in the Bible is so large," declares Walter Kaiser, "and their distribution so evenly spread through both Testaments and all types of literary forms that the interpreter is alerted to the fact that he or she is dealing with a major component of the Bible."[2] Dr. Kaiser reports that the late Dr. J. Barton Payne calculated that 27 percent of the Bible deals with prophecy. Only the books of Ruth and Song of Solomon in the Old Testament, and the tiny epistles of Philemon and 3 John in the New Testament have no prophetic portions.

> The highest percentages of predictive material are found in the small books of Zephaniah (89 percent), Obadiah (81 percent), and Nahum (74 percent). In the New Testament, the honors go to Revelation (63 percent), Hebrews (45 percent), and 2 Peter (41 percent).[3]

Dr. W.H. Griffith-Thomas has noted that one out of twelve verses in the New Testament deal with the second coming. In the epistles, he says the second coming is found in one out of ten verses. Such preoccupation by God in His Word on this subject is hardly something that should be relegated to the back burner. How we view prophecy and the second coming will greatly impact our view of present Christian living.

What are some of the more prominent texts on the second coming? They include: Deuteronomy 30:3; Psalm 2; Isaiah 63:1-6; Daniel 2:44,45; 7:13,14; Zechariah 14:1-4; Matthew 24–25; Mark 13; Luke 21; Acts 1:9-11; Romans 11:26; 1 Thessalonians 3:13; 5:1-4; 2 Thessalonians 1:6–2:12; 2 Peter 2:1–3:17; Jude 14,15; Revelation 1:7; 19:11-21.

The first prophetic passage regarding the second coming is found in Deuteronomy 30:1-5:

> So it shall be when all of these things have come upon you, the blessing and the curse which I have set before you, and

The Truth About Christ's Second Coming 9

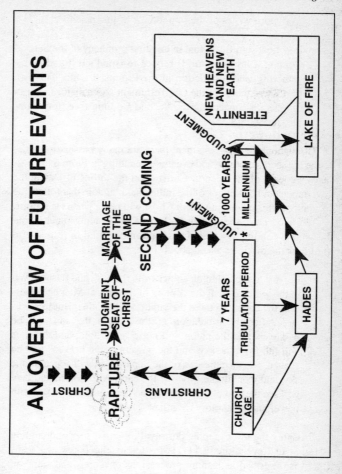

you call them to mind in all nations where the LORD your God has banished you, and you return to the LORD your God and obey Him with all your heart and soul according to all that I command you today, you and your sons, then the LORD your God will restore you from captivity, and have compassion on you, and will gather you again from all the peoples where the LORD your God has scattered you.

If your outcasts are at the ends of the earth, from there the LORD your God will gather you, and from there He will bring you back. And the LORD your God will bring you into the land which your fathers possessed, and you shall possess it; and He will prosper you and multiply you more than your fathers.

Dr. Walvoord writes of the importance of this passage:

> It is most significant that in this first prophecy of the Second Coming, Christ's return is related to Israel's restoration, regathering, and installation in the Promised Land. This is a prominent theme of the Old Testament and a major factor in prophecies concerning the Second Coming (see, for example, Jer. 23:5-8).[4]

Throughout the Old Testament there are many passages that describe the second coming and events surrounding it. From these passages we learn of the reign of Christ upon the throne of David, the government and conditions of the millennial kingdom that follow the second coming, and the judgment Christ will bring when He returns.

While on earth the first time, Jesus Christ taught much about the second coming. One vivid description occurred in response to questions the disciples asked about the event:

> For just as the lightning comes from the east, and flashes even to the west, so shall the coming of the Son of Man be. Wherever the corpse is, there the vultures will gather. But immediately after the tribulation of those days the sun will be darkened, and the moon will not give its light, and the stars will fall from the sky, and the powers of the heavens will be shaken, and then the sign of the Son of Man will appear in the sky, and then all the tribes of the earth will mourn, and they will see the Son of Man coming on the clouds of the sky with power and great glory (Matthew 24:27-30).

Probably the most graphic portrayal of Christ's second coming is found in Revelation 19:11-21. In this extended passage Jesus Christ is described as leading processions of angels and saints in heaven to claim the earth, destroy the armies of the world, and defeat the Antichrist and False Prophet.[5]

> And I saw heaven opened; and behold, a white horse, and He who sat upon it is called Faithful and True; and in righteousness He judges and wages war. And His eyes are a flame of fire, and upon His head are many diadems; and He has a name written upon Him which no one knows except Himself. And He is clothed with a robe dipped in blood; and His name is called The Word of God. And the armies which are in heaven, clothed in fine linen, white and clean, were following Him on white horses. And from His mouth comes a sharp sword, so that with it He may smite the nations; and He will rule them with a rod of iron; and He treads the wine

press of the fierce wrath of God, the Almighty. And on His robe and on His thigh He has a name written, "KING OF KINGS, AND LORD OF LORDS."

> And I saw an angel standing in the sun; and he cried out with a loud voice, saying to all the birds which fly in midheaven, "Come, assemble for the great supper of God; in order that you may eat the flesh of kings and the flesh of commanders and the flesh of mighty men and the flesh of horses and of those who sit on them and the flesh of all men, both free men and slaves, and small and great." And I saw the beast and the kings of the earth and their armies, assembled to make war against Him who sat upon the horse, and against His army. And the beast was seized, and with him the false prophet who performed the signs in his presence, by which he deceived those who had received the mark of the beast and those who worshiped his image; these two were thrown alive into the lake of fire which burns with brimstone. And the rest were killed with the sword which came from the mouth of Him who sat upon the horse, and all the birds were filled with their flesh.

This passage shows that Christ's return will be one that entails great physical destruction and many deaths. For those who are not Christ's own, it will be a terrifying time.

2. What is the relationship between Christ's first and second coming?

The Bible depicts the career of Christ as revolving around two major aspects. Titus 2:11-14 speaks of Christ's two appearances on earth. The first phase is related to His coming to suffer humiliation and to die for the sins of mankind. The second phase is when He will come in power and glory to reign over all mankind.

> For the grace of God has appeared, bringing salvation to all men, instructing us to deny ungodliness and worldly desires and to live sensibly, righteously and godly in the present age, looking for the blessed hope and the appearing of the glory of our great God and Savior, Christ Jesus; who gave Himself for us, that He might redeem us from every lawless deed and purify for Himself a people for His own possession, zealous for good deeds.

Philippians provides great insight into the purpose of Christ's two advents:

> Have this attitude in yourselves which was also in Christ Jesus, who, although He existed in the form of God, did not regard equality with God a thing to be grasped, but emptied Himself, taking the form of a bond-servant, and being made in the likeness of men. And being found in appearance as a man, He humbled Himself by becoming obedient to the point of death, even death on a cross. Therefore also God highly exalted Him, and bestowed on Him the name which is above every name, that at the name of Jesus EVERY KNEE SHOULD BOW, of those who are in heaven, and on earth, and under the earth, and that every tongue should confess that Jesus Christ is Lord, to the glory of God the Father (Philippians 2:5-11).

Hebrews 9:28 explains and contrasts Christ's two comings: "So Christ also, having been offered once to bear the sins of many, shall appear a second time for salvation without reference to sin, to those who eagerly await Him."

3. Is the second coming physical or spiritual?

The second coming of Christ is a physical return that will be clearly visible to all. His first coming to earth was physical, and so will be the second coming. Dr. Walvoord writes:

> Though it is true that Christ is present everywhere and indwells every Christian, bodily he has remained in heaven. At the Second Coming he will return bodily to earth. Just as the Ascension was a bodily ascension into heaven, so the Second Coming will be a bodily return to earth. The angels who met the disciples after the ascension of Christ told them, "This same Jesus, who has been taken from you into heaven, will come back in the same way you have seen him go into heaven" (Acts 1:11). Jesus went into heaven bodily and visibly in the clouds. His second coming will have all these same characteristics.[6]

If Christ's second coming was merely spiritual it would not be a *second* coming. What do we mean? Christ has already come spiritually in the form of His indwelling presence and through the Holy Spirit. For Him to come again is contrasted with His first coming, which was also physical. Thus, His second coming can only be thought of as a bodily coming.

4. What biblical terms are used to refer to the second coming?

The specific phrase *second coming* doesn't appear in the Bible; however Hebrews 9:28 does tell us that Christ "shall appear a second

The Truth About Christ's Second Coming 13

time." Nevertheless, there are many words and concepts that are synonyms for "second coming" or refer to it. In the New Testament many of these terms speak of Christ's coming as well as the rapture, even though they are separate events. A study of the context determines which a given writer has in mind.

Second Coming Words and Verses

apokalupsis—"an uncovering," "laying bare," "a revealing, revelation": ". . . and to give relief to you who are afflicted and to us as well when the Lord Jesus shall *be revealed* from heaven with His mighty angels in flaming fire" (2 Thessalonians 1:7). (Verb also used in 1 Peter 4:13.)

erchomai—"to come or to appear": "Jesus said to them, 'You have said it yourself; nevertheless I tell you, hereafter you shall see THE SON OF MAN SITTING AT THE RIGHT HAND OF POWER, and *COMING* ON THE CLOUDS OF HEAVEN'" (Matthew 26:64). (Verb also used in Mark 14:62; Luke 21:27; Acts 1:11; Revelation 1:7; 22:7,12,20.)

parousia—"a being present, presence," "a coming," "an arrival": "And then that lawless one will be revealed whom the Lord will slay with the breath of His mouth and bring to an end by the appearance of His *coming*" (2 Thessalonians 2:8). (Verb also used in 1 Thessalonians 3:13.)

Rapture Words and Verses

harpazó—"caught up," "to seize upon with force," "to snatch up": "Then we who are alive and remain shall be *caught up* together with them in the clouds to meet the Lord in the air, and thus we shall always be with the Lord" (1 Thessalonians 4:17).

episunagógé—"gathering together," "assembly": "Now we request you, brethren, with regard to the coming of our Lord Jesus Christ, and our *gathering together* to Him" (2 Thessalonians 2:1).

allassó—"to change," "to transform," "to exchange": "Behold, I tell you a mystery; we shall not all sleep, but we shall all be *changed*, in a moment, in the twinkling of an eye, at the last trumpet; for the trumpet will sound, and the dead will be raised imperishable, and we will be *changed*" (1 Corinthians 15:51,52).

paralambanó—"to take to," "to receive to oneself": "If I go and prepare a place for you, I will come again, and *receive* you to Myself; that where I am, there you may be also" (John 14:3).

epiphaneia—"a manifestation," "an appearance": ". . . looking for the blessed hope and *the appearing* of the glory of our great God and Savior, Christ Jesus" (Titus 2:13).

14 *The Truth About Christ's Second Coming*

rhuomai—"to draw to oneself," "to rescue," "to deliver": ". . . and to wait for His Son from heaven, whom He raised from the dead, that is Jesus, who ***delivers*** us from the wrath to come" (1 Thessalonians 1:10).

apokalupsis—"an uncovering," "laying bare," "a revealing, revelation": "Therefore, gird your minds for action, keep sober in spirit, fix your hope completely on the grace to be brought to you at ***the revelation*** of Jesus Christ" (1 Peter 1:13).

parousia—"a being present, presence," "a coming," "an arrival": "Be patient, therefore, brethren, until ***the coming*** of the Lord. Behold, the farmer waits for the precious produce of the soil, being patient about it, until it gets the early and late rains. You too be patient; strengthen your hearts, for ***the coming*** of the Lord is at hand" (James 5:7,8).

From the samples above, it is clear that there are distinct words and words that overlap for the two appearings of Christ. This is not always readily apparent in our English translations.

PART 2

What Is the Purpose of the Second Coming?

5. Why is the second coming necessary?

The second coming of Jesus Christ to the earth is one of the major events in the Bible. Hebrews 9:28 says, "So Christ also . . . shall appear a second time for salvation without reference to sin, to those who eagerly await Him." Jesus Christ is coming again to vanquish His enemies and to reign in righteousness upon this earth for 1,000 years. The second coming will end the tribulation and begin the millennium.

One of the purposes of the second coming is to right wrongs that have occurred throughout history. Many injustices have been done to God's people that have not been vindicated. God will avenge His people at the second coming (2 Thessalonians 2:5-10). The second coming enables believers to not become overwhelmed by injustice because they know that perfect justice will be executed at Christ's return. Dr. Walvoord explains:

> According to Revelation 19:15, Christ's purpose is to judge the world: "Out of his mouth comes a sharp sword with which to strike down the nations. 'He will rule them with an iron scepter.' He treads the winepress of the fury of the wrath of God Almighty." On his robe and on his thigh he

has this name written: KING OF KINGS AND LORD OF LORDS (v. 16). The events that follow first portray the judgment on the enemies of God, then on the Beast and the False Prophet, and finally on Satan. Other Scriptures indicate that judgment will extend to the entire living population on the earth. In his second coming Christ will terminate his time of waiting on the throne of God for the future subjugation of his enemies. He will then judge the world and bring everything under his authority and power. Noteworthy is the fact that there is no mention of the rapture of living saints in this sequence. This will have occurred years before.[7]

The specific setting for Christ's second advent will be related to the campaign of Armageddon. Christ will have gathered the armies of the world to Israel through the sixth bowl judgment (Revelation 16:12-16). Next, Christ will judge and destroy Babylon in one hour as the whole earth mourns (Revelation 18:10,11). The Antichrist will then send his armies to surround and attack Jerusalem (Zechariah 12:1-9; 14:1,2). He will also send his forces to Bozrah, or Petra, in southern Jordan, where many of the Jews would have fled since the middle of the tribulation (Jeremiah 49:13,14; Micah 2:12). These events will then trigger the national regeneration and conversion of Israel three days before the second coming (Hosea 6:1-3; Zechariah 12:10-14; Romans 11:25-27).

Because of these circumstances, a now-converted Israel will plea for Messiah—Jesus of Nazerath—to come and rescue the Jews from the impossible situation of Armageddon that they find themselves in. The second coming is in essence a rescue event. Christ returns first to Bozrah and rescues Israel from the Antichrist and his armies (Isaiah 14:3-21; Jeremiah 49:20-22; Joel 3:12,13; Zechariah 14:12-15; Revelation 14:19,20). After this Christ makes His victory descent to the Mount of Olives in Jerusalem (Joel 3:14-17; Zechariah 14:3-5; Matthew 24:29,30). The second coming will be completed at that point.

6. How does Israel relate to the second coming?

In some ways the second coming is all about Israel. The purpose of the second coming is to rescue Israel from the nations of the world who surrounded it at Armageddon. Israel will itself face annihilation by the armies of the world who are motivated by Satan himself. Therefore, God's nation will need direct, divine intervention. This she will receive when, after conversion to Jesus as her Messiah, she calls upon the Lord for salvation (Zechariah 12:10; Matthew 23:39; Romans 11:25-27).

Dr. Walvoord further explains Israel's relationship and role in the second coming:

> The second advent is not only an important event in itself of tremendous significance, but its relationships extend to every important undertaking of God related to the end time.
>
> *Relation to Israel* . . . At this coming of Christ, Israel is delivered from her enemies and persecutions which characterized the time of Jacob's trouble just prior to the second advent. It also is the time in which Israel is brought into the millennial reign, which is a time of deliverance, glory and blessing for the nation. This deliverance is indicated in many passages such as Joel 2; Matthew 24–25; Romans 11:26; and Revelation 19:17-21. Zechariah 14:1-3 indicates that Jerusalem itself in the midst of military conflict will be rescued by the return of the Lord.
>
> The second coming of Christ also will be the occasion for Israel's judgment. Those who survive the tribulation will be judged concerning their relationship to Christ and those who are worthy to enter the kingdom will be brought into the promised land while others will be purged out (Ezek. 20:34-38; Matt. 24:9–25:30). It is probable that the judgment of Israel raised from the dead also will take place at this time and Israel will be rewarded (Dan. 12:2-3).
>
> Those Israelites living on earth who qualify for entrance into the kingdom are brought into the land promised to their fathers and fulfill extended passages of prophecy relating to the regathering, revival and restoration of the nation Israel (Isa. 25:9-10; 27:12-13; 61:3–62:12; 65:8–66:24; Jer. 23:1-40; 31:1-40; 33:1-26; Ezek. 33:21–37:28; 40:1–48:25; Dan. 2:44-45; 7:9-27; Zech. 13:8-9; Rom. 11:26; Rev. 20:4).[8]

The second coming will be the highlight of Israel's history. She will finally be vindicated; her enemies will be destroyed. She will become converted to Jesus as Messiah and will have the many promises of blessing fulfilled. In many ways the second coming will be the beginning for the nation of Israel, not the end.

7. How do the nations relate to the second coming?

The whole world will be affected by the second coming; therefore, all the Gentile nations will be involved in this grand event. Matthew 25:31-46 teaches that Christ will judge all Gentiles at the second coming:

But when the Son of Man comes in His glory, and all the angels with Him, then He will sit on His glorious throne. And all the nations will be gathered before Him; and He will separate them from one another, as the shepherd separates the sheep from the goats; and He will put the sheep on His right, and the goats on the left.

Dr. Walvoord summarizes God's plan for the Gentile nations:

The second coming marks the important transition from the times of the Gentiles to the millennial kingdom of Christ and ends the period beginning with the captivity of Israel in the seventh century B.C. As Daniel's prophecies indicate, four great world empires run their course, culminating in the final world empire which will rule the world at the time of the great tribulation. This empire of the end times constitutes the final portion of the fourth empire.

The second coming of Christ is the occasion for the judgment of the Gentiles, both nationally and individually (Ezek. 38:1–39:29; Dan. 2:44-45; Matt. 25:31-46; Rev. 19:15). This judgment is specifically directed to Gentiles living at the second coming. Gentiles who have put their faith in Christ are ushered into the blessings of the millennial kingdom and all others are put to death.[9]

8. How does the church relate to the second coming?

The church will have been raptured to heaven to be with the Lord more than seven years before the second coming. At the second coming, the Bible teaches that the church—the bride of Christ clothed in fine linen—will return from heaven to earth with Christ:

It was given to her to clothe herself in fine linen, bright and clean; for the fine linen is the righteous acts of the saints. . . . And the armies which are in heaven, clothed in fine linen, white and clean, were following Him on white horses (Revelation 19:8,14).

The New Testament teaches that Christ will right the wrongs at His return. Because of this we can endure suffering and persecution in the present.

This is a plain indication of God's righteous judgment so that you may be considered worthy of the kingdom of God, for which indeed you are suffering. For after all it is only just for God to repay with affliction those who afflict you, and to give relief to you who are afflicted and to us as well when the Lord Jesus shall be revealed from heaven with His mighty angels in flaming fire, dealing out retribution to those who do not know God and to those who do not obey the gospel of our Lord Jesus. And these will pay the penalty of eternal destruction, away from the presence of the Lord and from the glory of His power, when He comes to be glorified in His saints on that day, and to be marveled at among all who have believed—for our testimony to you was believed (2 Thessalonians 1:5-10).

9. How does creation relate to the second coming?

After having been virtually destroyed because of God's war on man's sin, the creation will be restored at the second coming. Christ will remove the curse, except death (which will go after the millennium), that came as a result of Adam's sin (see Genesis 3). Dr. Walvoord summarizes:

> When Christ returns to the earth there is also a dramatic change in creation as a whole. A curse which fell upon the physical world as a result of Adam's sin is now at least partially relieved and the natural world is restored to the fruitfulness and Edenic beauty it had before the fall (Isa. 11:6-8; 35:1-10; 65:18-25; Rom. 8:21-22). As a result of the removal of the curse the desert will be reclaimed, water will be found in the wilderness, and prosperity will characterize the earth. The fact that the earth is abundant in its fruitfulness contributes immeasurably to the prosperity and blessing which characterize Christ's reign on the earth.[10]

10. How do sin and Satan relate to the second coming?

The second coming of Christ will include the greatest arrest in history—Satan's. Satan will be put out of circulation for 1,000 years, which will result in a huge decline in social, religious, economic, and political evil. However, at the end of the millennium, after a brief revolt, Satan will join the rest of the fallen angels in the lake of fire for eternity. Dr. Walvoord says,

> As plainly stated in Revelation 20:1-3 Satan is bound and rendered inoperative at the beginning of the millennial reign of Christ. It may be assumed that at the same time all

The Truth About Christ's Second Coming 19

demonic activity will cease. As Christ will be reigning with absolute authority over the world, no open wickedness will be permitted and any sin or rebellion against Christ will be immediately judged and put down (Isa. 11:3-5). While human beings in their natural bodies on earth will still have a sin nature capable of falling short of the perfect will of God, there will be no stimulus of this by Satan or evil spirits, and whatever sin eventuates will be due solely to the evil heart of man. This situation makes possible a world in which all people at least outwardly profess to follow the Saviour, and civilization as a whole attains an unusually high standard of morality and spirituality. Only at the end of the millennium when Satan is again loosed is there rebellion against Christ resulting in judgment upon those who join hands with Satan (Rev. 20:7-10).[11]

Sin will be greatly reduced at the second coming, but not eliminated until the end of the millennium when the new heavens and the new earth will be created. Sin cannot totally be removed until this current cursed earth is judged and destroyed; only when this world is regenerated will sin be totally done away.

11. What are the major events surrounding the second coming?

One of the major occurrences leading up to the second coming is the battle of Armageddon. How does this event unfold? Dr. Arnold Fruchtenbaum has identified eight major events:[12]

- The First Stage: The assembling of the allies of the Antichrist (Revelation 16:12-16).

- The Second Stage: The destruction of Babylon in one hour (Revelation 18:15-18).

- The Third Stage: The fall of Jerusalem to the army of the Antichrist (Micah 4:11–5:1; Zechariah 12:1-3; 14:1,2).

- The Fourth Stage: The armies of the Antichrist move to annihilate the Jews in Bozrah (Petra) (Jeremiah 49:13,14; Micah 2:12).

- The Fifth Stage: The national regeneration of Israel leading to Israel's confession of sin and acceptance of Jesus as her Messiah (Isaiah 53:1-9; Zechariah 12:10; Matthew 23:37-39; Romans 11:25-27, etc.).

- The Sixth Stage: The second coming of Jesus beginning with the rescue of the Jews at Bozrah after Israel's invitation (Isaiah 34:1-7; 63:1-6; Habakkuk 3:3; Micah 2:12,13; Zechariah 12:7).

- The Seventh Stage: The conflict from Bozrah to the valley of Jehoshaphat commonly known as the battle of Armageddon (Isaiah 14:3-21; Jeremiah 49:20-22; Habakkuk 3:13; Zechariah 14:12-15; Revelation 17–21).

- The Eighth Stage: The second coming or victory ascent upon the Mount of Olives (Joel 3:14-17; Zechariah 14:3-5; Matthew 24:29-31; Revelation 19:11-21).

12. Where will the second coming occur?

In the first chapter of Acts we read of the ascent of Jesus from the Mount of Olives after the resurrection and 40 days with the disciples. As the disciples stood watching the ascent, two angels appeared telling them: "Men of Galilee, why do you stand looking into the sky? This Jesus, who has been taken up from you into heaven, will come in just the same way as you have watched Him go into heaven" (Acts 1:11).

The return of Christ, or the second coming (not the rapture), was prophesied by Zechariah almost 600 years earlier: "And in that day His feet will stand on the Mount of Olives, which is in front of Jerusalem on the east; and the Mount of Olives will be split in its middle from east to west by a very large valley, so that half of the mountain will move toward the north and the other half toward the south" (Zechariah 14:4). Since Christ delivered His great prophetic discourse on His second coming from the Mount of Olives, it is clearly implied that His return will be to the same location (Matthew 24–25). It is at this site that He will make his victory ascent after defeating the Antichrist and his forces.

Sixty years after the ascension, the apostle John also wrote of Christ's second coming to earth, although the Mount of Olives is not mentioned specifically (see Revelation 19:11-16). Remember, this coming should not be confused with the rapture that occurs seven years earlier and is recorded in 1 Thessalonians 4:14-17. These two comings are separate and distinct events.

The return of Christ to Jerusalem will be for the purpose of judging the world, establishing His millennial kingdom, and reigning on the throne of David in fulfillment of Old Testament prophecies that assured a Messiah-king for Israel from the Davidic line. While Christ's reign will be universal, He will rule from Jerusalem because of the Davidic throne and the spiritual restoration of Israel. Dr. Walvoord writes:

> His reign over the house of Israel will be from Jerusalem (Isa. 2:1-4), and from the same location he will also reign as King of Kings and Lord of Lords over the entire earth (Ps. 72:8-11,17-19).... The Millennium will be the occasion of the final restoration of Israel. At the beginning of the millennial kingdom Israel will experience her final and permanent regathering (Ezek. 39:25-29; Amos 9:15). Christ's reign over Israel will be glorious and will be a complete and literal fulfillment of all that God promised David (Jer. 23:5-8).[13]

No other city or location on earth would permit the fulfillment of prophecy or allow for the rule and restoration of Israel. Jerusalem's biblical, prophetic, and worldwide significance will continue and be increased at the second coming of Christ.

P A R T 3

When Will the Second Coming Occur?

13. Are the rapture and the second coming simultaneous?

The rapture and the second coming are separate events in character and timing. A pretribulational perspective has them clearly separated by the seven-year tribulation. The prophetic timeline of Daniel 9:24-27 and 2 Thessalonians 2 places the tribulation after the rapture and just before the second coming. There are some Christians who believe that the rapture and second coming will occur after the tribulation and either simultaneously or very close together. This position is known as posttribulationism. However, careful and consistent observation of the biblical distinctions, terminology, history, and nuances leads to a pretribulational perspective that clearly distinguishes the two events.

14. Why are the rapture and the second coming separate events?

Dr. John Feinberg notes that distinguishing between the rapture and second coming is important in establishing pretribulationism against the nonpretribulational claim that the Bible does not teach such a view:

22   *The Truth About Christ's Second Coming*

> The pretribulationist must show that there is enough dissimilarity between clear rapture and clear second advent passages as to warrant the claim that the two kinds of passages *could* be speaking about two events which *could* occur at different times. The pretribulationist does not have to prove at this point . . . that the two events must occur at different times, but only that the exegetical data from rapture and second advent passages do not make it impossible for the events to occur at different times. If he can do that, the pretribulationist has shown that his view is not impossible. And, he has answered the posttribulationist's strongest line of evidence.[14]

A key factor in understanding the New Testament's teaching of the pretribulational rapture revolves around the fact that two future comings of Christ are presented. The first coming is the catching up into the clouds of the church before the seven-year tribulation, and the second coming occurs at the end of the tribulation when Christ returns to the earth to begin His 1,000-year kingdom. Anyone desirous of insight into the biblical teaching of the rapture and second advent must study and decide whether Scripture speaks of one or two future events.

Framing the Issue

Posttribulationists usually contend that if the rapture and the second coming are two distinct events, separated by about seven years, then there ought to be at least one passage in Scripture that clearly teaches this. However, the Bible doesn't always teach God's truth in accordance with our preconceived notions or in such a way that answers directly all of our questions. For example, a Unitarian could design a similar kind of question regarding the trinity: "Where is at least one passage in Scripture that clearly says that the Persons of the Godhead are distinct?" We who believe the trinity reply that the Bible teaches the trinity but in a different way.

Many important biblical doctrines are not given to us directly from a single verse; we often need to harmonize passages into systematic conclusions. Some truths are directly stated in the Bible, such as the deity of Christ (John 1:1; Titus 2:13). But doctrines like the trinity and the incarnate nature of Christ are the product of biblical unity. Taking into account all biblical texts, orthodox theologians over time recognized that God is a trinity and that Christ is the God-Man. Similarly, a systematic consideration of all biblical passages reveals that Scripture teaches two future comings.

Posttribulationists often contend that the pretribulational position is built merely upon an assumption that certain verses "make sense" if and only if the pretribulational model of the rapture is assumed to be correct. However, they often fail to make it clear to their readers that they are just as dependent upon assumptions. Their error stems from failure to observe actual biblical distinctions.

For example, Christ's ministry has two phases that revolve around His two comings. *Phase one* took place at Christ's first coming when He came in humility to suffer. *Phase two* will begin at Christ's second coming when He will reign on earth in power and glory. Failure to distinguish these two phases was a key factor in Israel's rejection of Jesus as Messiah. In the same way, failure to see clear distinctions between the rapture and second advent lead many to a misinterpretation of God's future plan.

The Nature of the Rapture

The rapture is most clearly presented in 1 Thessalonians 4:13-18. It is characterized as a "translation coming" (1 Corinthians 15:51,52; 1 Thessalonians 4:15-17) in which Christ comes *for* His church. The second advent is Christ returning with His saints, descending from heaven to establish His earthly kingdom (Zechariah 14:4,5; Matthew 24:27-31). Dr. Ed Hindson observes:

> The rapture (or "translation") of the church is often paralleled to the "raptures" of Enoch (Genesis 5:24) and Elijah (2 Kings 2:12). In each case, the individual disappeared or was caught up into heaven. At His ascension, our Lord Himself was "taken up" into heaven (Acts 1:9). The biblical description of the rapture involves both the resurrection of deceased believers and the translation of living believers into the air to meet the Lord (1 Thessalonians 4:16-17; 1 Corinthians 15:51-52).[15]

Differences between the two events are harmonized naturally by the pretribulational position, while other views are not able to account comfortably for such distinctions.

Dr. John Walvoord concludes that these "contrasts should make it evident that the translation of the church is an event quite different in character and time from the return of the Lord to establish His kingdom, and confirms the conclusion that the translation takes place before the tribulation."[16]

Additional Differences

Paul speaks of the rapture as a mystery (1 Corinthians 15:51-54), a truth not revealed until its disclosure by the apostles (Colossians 1:26). This makes the rapture a separate event because the

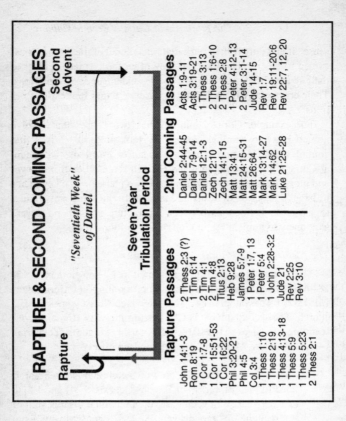

RAPTURE & SECOND COMING PASSAGES

Rapture — "Seventieth Week" of Daniel / Seven-Year Tribulation Period — **Second Advent**

Rapture Passages

John 14:1-3
Rom 8:19
1 Cor 1:7-8
1 Cor 15:51-53
1 Cor 16:22
Phil 3:20-21
Col 3:4
1 Thess 1:10
1 Thess 2:19
1 Thess 4:13-18
1 Thess 5:9
1 Thess 5:23
2 Thess 2:1
2 Thess 2:3 (?)
1 Tim 6:14
2 Tim 4:1
2 Tim 4:8
Titus 2:13
Heb 9:28
James 5:7-9
1 Peter 1:7, 13
1 Peter 5:4
1 John 2:28-3:2
Jude 21
Rev 2:25
Rev 3:10

2nd Coming Passages

Daniel 2:44-45
Daniel 7:9-14
Daniel 12:1-3
Zech 12:10
Zech 14:1-15
Matt 13:41
Matt 24:15-31
Matt 26:64
Mark 13:14-27
Mark 14:62
Luke 21:25-28
Acts 1:9-11
Acts 3:19-21
1 Thess 3:13
2 Thess 1:6-10
2 Thess 2:8
1 Peter 4:12-13
2 Peter 3:1-14
Jude 14-15
Rev 1:7
Rev 19:11-20:6
Rev 22:7, 12, 20

Rapture/Translation	Second Coming Established Kingdom
1. Translation of all believers	1. No translation at all
2. Translated saints go to heaven	2. Translated saints return to earth
3. Earth not judged	3. Earth judged and righteousness established
4. Imminent, any-moment, signless	4. Follows definite predicted signs, including tribulation
5. Not in the Old Testament	5. Predicted often in Old Testament
6. Believers only	6. Affects all people
7. Before the day of wrath	7. Concluding the day of wrath
8. No reference to Satan	8. Satan bound
9. Christ comes *for* His own	9. Christ comes *with* His own
10. He comes in the *air*	10. He comes to the *earth*
11. He claims His bride	11. He comes with His bride
12. Only His own see Him	12. Every eye shall see Him
13. Tribulation begins	13. Millennial kingdom begins

second coming was predicted in the Old Testament (Daniel 12:1-3; Zechariah 12:10; 14:4).

The movement for the believer at the rapture is from earth to heaven, while it is from heaven to earth at the second advent. At the rapture the Lord comes only for believers, but His return to the earth will impact all people. The rapture is a translation/resurrection event where the Lord takes believers "to the Father's house" in heaven (see John 14:3), while at the second coming believers return from heaven to the earth (Matthew 24:30). Hindson says, "The different aspects of our Lord's return are clearly delineated in the Scriptures themselves. The only real issue in the eschatological debate is the time *interval* between them."[17]

The distinctions between Christ's coming in the air to rapture His church are too great to be reduced into a single coming at the end of the tribulation. These biblical distinctions provide a strong basis for the pretribulational rapture.

As Christians await the fulfillment of Bible prophecy and both the rapture and second coming, there should not be an attitude of apathy. We must remember that both events will be surrounded by death, destruction, tragedy, terror, grief, and despair for those who don't know Jesus Christ. Christians are not to be gleeful or gloating about either event. Rather, we should be serious and sincere. To be sure, we should have no fear of the coming storm, but neither should we deny its ramifications. Writing of a proper attitude toward the rapture, Dr. Walvoord observes:

> The revelation of the prophetic Word was not designed simply to comfort and to enlighten. The hope of the Lord's return should constitute an impelling challenge. The task is large and the days are few. It is time for searching of heart and purification of life. It is time for prayer and devotion, for sacrifice and effort. Now is the time to preach the good news of a Savior who died for the sins of the whole world that all who believe might live. It is a time to press on through closing missionary doors, through opposition, unbelief, and indifference. It is time to remind ourselves of that searching evaluation of our life and labors that awaits us at the judgment seat of Christ. The coming of the Lord is as near as our next breath, the next beat of our hearts, the next word of our lips. While we wait, may we be "steadfast, unmovable, always abounding in the work of the Lord" (1 Cor. 15:58).[18]

15. Why is an interval necessary between the rapture and the second coming?

A gap of time is needed between the rapture and the second coming in order to facilitate in a timely manner many events predicted in the Bible. Numerous items in the New Testament can be attuned by a pretrib time gap of at least seven years, while other views, especially posttribulationists, are forced to postulate scenarios that would not realistically allow for normal passage of time. The following events are best temporally harmonized with an interval of time as put forth by pretribulationism.[19]

- Second Corinthians 5:10 teaches that all believers of this age must appear before the judgment seat of Christ in heaven. This event, often known as the bema judgment from the Greek word *bema*, is an event never mentioned in the detailed accounts connected with the second coming of Christ to the earth. Since such an evaluation would require some passage of time, the pretrib gap of seven years nicely accounts for such a requirement.

- Revelation 19:7-10 pictures the church as a bride who has been made ready for marriage (illustrated as "fine linen," which represents "the righteous acts of the saints") to her groom (Christ). The bride has already been clothed in preparation for her return at the second coming when she accompanies Christ to the earth (Revelation 19:11-18). It follows that the church would already have to be complete and in heaven (because of the pretrib rapture) in order to have been prepared in the way that Revelation 19 describes. This requires an interval of time which pretribulationism handles well.

- The 24 elders of Revelation 4:1–5:14 are best understood as representatives of the church. Dr. Charles Ryrie explains:

In the New Testament, elders as the highest officials in the church do represent the whole church (cf. Acts 15:6; 20:28), and in the Old Testament, twenty-four elders were appointed by King David to represent the entire Levitical priesthood (1 Chron. 24). When those twenty-four elders met together in the temple precincts in Jerusalem, the entire priestly house was represented. Thus it seems more likely that the elders represent redeemed human beings . . . the church is included and is thus in heaven before the tribulation begins.[20]

If they refer to the church, then this would necessitate the rapture and reward of the church *before* the tribulation and would require a chronological gap for them to perform their heavenly duties during the seven-year tribulation.

The Truth About Christ's Second Coming   27

- Believers who come to faith in Christ during the tribulation are not translated at Christ's second advent but carry on ordinary occupations such as farming and building houses, and they will bear children (Isaiah 65:20-25). This would be impossible if all saints were translated at the second coming to the earth, as posttribulationists teach. Because pretribulationists have at least a seven-year interval between the removal of the church at the rapture and the return of Christ to the earth, this is not a problem because millions of people will be saved during the interval and thus be available to populate the millennium in their natural bodies in order to fulfill Scripture.

- It would be impossible for the judgment of the Gentiles to take place after the second coming if the rapture and second coming are not separated by a gap of time. How would both saved and unsaved, still in their natural bodies, be separated in judgment if all living believers are translated at the second coming? This problem is solved through a pretribulational gap.

- Dr. John F. Walvoord points out that if "the translation took place in connection with the second coming to the earth, there would be no need of separating the sheep from the goats at a subsequent judgment, but the separation would have taken place in the very act of the translation of the believers before Christ actually sets up His throne on earth (Matt. 25:31)."[21] Once again, such a problem is solved by taking a pretrib position with its gap of at least seven years.

- A time interval is needed so that God's program for the church, a time when Jew and Gentile are united in one body (see Ephesians 2–3), will not become commingled in any way with His unfinished and future plan for Israel during the tribulation. Dr. Renald Showers notes:

   All other views of the Rapture have the church going through at least part of the 70th week, meaning that all other views mix God's 70-weeks program for Israel and Jerusalem together with His program for the church.[22]

A gap is needed in order for these two aspects of God's program to be harmonized in a nonconflicting manner.

The pretribulational rapture of the church fulfills a biblical need to not only see a distinction between the translation of church-age saints at the rapture, before the second coming, but it also handles without difficulty the necessity of a time-gap which harmonizes a number of future biblical events. This requirement of a seven-year gap of time adds another plank to the likelihood that pretribulationism best reflects the biblical viewpoint.

16. Are there signs for the second coming?

While the rapture is a signless event, there will be dozens of signs leading up to the second coming after the rapture. Some of these include: the signing of a covenant between the Antichrist and Israel (Daniel 9:27); the two witnesses (Revelation 11:3); the 144,000 witnesses (Revelation 7:4); the events of the seven seal judgments (Revelation 6); the events of the trumpet (Revelation 8:6–10:7); the events of the bowl judgments (Revelation 16:2-17); the abomination of desolation in the rebuilt temple (Matthew 24:15); the issuing of the mark of the beast (Revelation 13:16,17); the three angelic announcements of Revelation 14; and the blackouts of the sun, moon, and stars (Revelation 6:12,13). Scripture says, "When these things begin to take place, straighten up and lift up your heads, because your redemption is drawing near" (Luke 21:28).

17. Has the second coming already occurred?

No, the second coming hasn't yet occurred even though there are some within Christendom who make such claims. This interpretation is known as preterism (Latin for "past"). Preterists argue that major prophetic portions of Scripture such as the Olivet Discourse (Matthew 24–25) and the book of Revelation were fulfilled in events surrounding the A.D. 70 destruction of Jerusalem by the Romans.

Not all preterists believe that the final second coming of Christ has occurred, but they all do believe that Christ has returned in some form. Extreme preterists, or consistent preterists as they prefer to be known, believe that all future Bible prophecy was fulfilled in the destruction of Jerusalem in A.D. 70. If there is a future second coming they believe the Bible doesn't talk about it. This puts them in the unorthodox position of not only denying the second coming but also the bodily resurrection of believers.

18. What is the relation between Armageddon and the second coming?

Armageddon will be the last great world war of history, which will take place in Israel in conjunction with the second coming of Christ. The battle or campaign of Armageddon is described in

Daniel 11:40-45; Joel 3:9-17; Zechariah 14:1-3; and Revelation 16:14-16. It will occur in the final days of the tribulation just before and in conjunction with the second coming of Christ. John tells us that the kings of the world will be gathered together "for the war of the great day of God, the Almighty" in a place known as "Har-Magedon" (see Revelation 16:14,16). The site for the converging of the armies is the plain of Esdraelon, around the hill of Megiddo. The area is located in northern Israel about 20 miles south-southeast of Haifa.

The term *Armageddon* comes from Hebrew. *Har* is the word for "mountain" and often appears with the Hebrew definite article "H." *Mageddon* is likely the ruins of an ancient city that overlooks the Valley of Esdraelon in Northern Israel. According to the Bible, great armies from the east and the west will assemble on this plain. There will be threats to the power of the Antichrist from the south, and he will also move to destroy a revived Babylon in the east before finally turning his forces toward Jerusalem to subdue and destroy it. As he and his armies move on Jerusalem, God will intervene and Jesus Christ will return to rescue His people, Israel. The Lord and His angelic army will destroy the armies, capture the Antichrist and the False Prophet, and cast them into the lake of fire (Revelation 19:11-21).

In a sense, Armageddon is a battle that never really takes place. That is, it doesn't take place in accordance with its original intent. Its human purpose is to execute the Antichrist's "final solution" to the "Jewish problem." This is why Jesus Christ chooses this moment in history for His return to earth—to thwart the Antichrist's attempted annihilation of the Jews and to destroy the armies of the world. It seems only fitting, in light of mankind's bloody legacy, that the return of Christ should be precipitated by worldwide military conflict against Israel.

PART 4

What Will Happen After the Second Coming?

19. Why does the millennium follow the second coming?

The millennium is the 1,000-year reign of Jesus Christ upon the earth after the tribulation, campaign of Armageddon, and the second coming. The most extensive New Testament passage regarding the millennium is Revelation 20, in which John describes the chronological sequence of the binding, rebellion, and judgment of Satan. Some prophecy scholars also hold that Revelation 21:9-27 describes the New Jerusalem during the millennium. This is not likely since it refers to the eternal state that is supported by

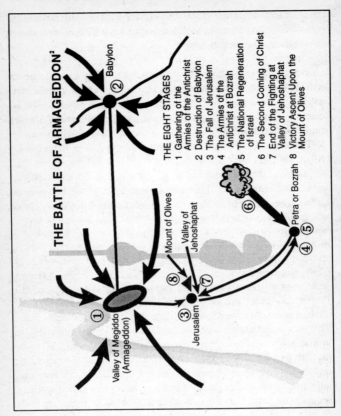

the sequential development of the text from the millennium in Revelation 20 to the eternal state in Revelation 21. Yet others hold a mediating position and see the passage as teaching the eternal habitation of resurrected saints during the millennium.[23]

The future kingdom of God will have two distinct phases: the millennium and the eternal state. However, the overwhelming emphasis of the Bible is upon the 1,000-year reign of Christ in the millennium. The millennium is a biblical reality that is yet to be realized. According to the Bible, life on earth will get better—but not before it gets worse during the seven-year tribulation.

In Psalm 2:6-9, the psalmist tells of the yet-future reign of Jesus Christ:

> But as for Me, I have installed My King upon Zion, My holy mountain. I will surely tell of the decree of the LORD: He said to Me, "Thou art My Son, today I have begotten Thee. Ask of Me, and I will surely give the nations as Thine in-

heritance, and the very ends of the earth as Thy possession. Thou shalt break them with a rod of iron, Thou shalt shatter them like earthenware."

An earthly kingdom with a physical presence and rule by the Messiah-King is foretold throughout the pages of Scripture. This promise was not fulfilled in the first coming of Jesus Christ because, though offered, the kingdom was rejected by Israel. Revelation 5 says that Christ is worthy to receive this kingdom, and in Revelation 11:15 we are told that the prophecies will yet be fulfilled. Dr. Charles Ryrie writes:

> Why is an earthly kingdom necessary? Did He not receive His inheritance when He was raised and exalted in heaven? Is not His present rule His inheritance? Why does there need to be an earthly kingdom? Because He must be triumphant *in the same arena* where He was seemingly defeated. His rejection by the rulers of this world was on this earth (1 Cor. 2:8). His exaltation must also be on this earth. And so it shall be when He comes again to rule this world in righteousness. He has waited long for His inheritance; soon He shall receive it.[24]

The millennium is a transitional period in God's program. It is the beginning of the eternal rule of God in the kingdom, which will pass into the eternal state. It is "the consummating link between history and the eternal order."[25] History and current events are moving toward a final era that will be the pinnacle of God's plan. Dr. David Larsen, citing the French theologian René Pache, writes:

> If history culminated with cataclysm and judgment, the Second Coming of Christ in power would be only "a walk through the ruins." The stone which becomes a mountain will "fill all the earth" (Daniel 2:35). "They will reign on earth" is the promise (Revelation 5:10). The venue of the Kingdom is to be on earth before we come to the final expression of the Kingdom in "the new heaven and the new earth" (2 Peter 3:13; Revelation 21–22).[26]

Both the second coming and the millennium are an integral part of God's plan for the future. Though they are different in purpose, they fall chronologically close on God's prophetic schedule.

20. What judgments occur at the second coming?

The second coming and its accompanying judgments occur just prior to the inauguration of the millennium. Just as Noah's flood

32 *The Truth About Christ's Second Coming*

was a bridge from the old world to the new, so the judgments at the second coming will be the cataclysmic hinge between our current era and the tribulation to the radically new conditions of the millennium. Thus, the second coming and the judgments that will accompany it are closely tied together. The judgments at the second coming "set the ball in motion" for the millennium to follow. These judgments will clean up the mess of previous human history so that the reign of Christ can commence. Regarding the relation of these two events, Dr. Walvoord observes:

> The millennial kingdom is a major part of the second coming of Christ. It includes the destruction of the armies gathered against God in the Holy Land (Rev. 19:17,21), the capture of the Beast and the False Prophet and their being cast into the lake of fire (v. 20), the binding of Satan (20:1-3), and the resurrection of the martyred dead of the Tribulation to reign with Christ a thousand years (vv. 4-6).[27]

The following are the specific judgments that occur either right before the second coming or at or shortly after His return:

- judgment of Babylon, the great harlot (Revelation 17–18; 19:2,3)
- judgment of the armies and nations at Armageddon (Revelation 19:11-21)
- judgment of the Gentile nations (Joel 3:1-3; Matthew 25:31-46)
- judgment of the beast or Antichrist (Revelation 19:19,20)
- judgment of the false prophet (Revelation 19:20)
- judgment of Satan (Revelation 20:1-3)
- judgment of Old Testament saints (Daniel 12:1-3)
- judgment of tribulation saints (Revelation 20:4-6)
- judgment of living Jews (Ezekiel 20:34-38)

21. Why is there a 75-day interval between the second coming and the millennium?

Careful reading of the Bible reveals that there is an interval of 75 days between the tribulation and the millennium. This interval comes at the end of the tribulation, after the second coming of Jesus Christ and the Armageddon conflict. In Daniel 12:11 mention is made of 1,290 days from the midpoint of the tribulation: "And from the time that the regular sacrifice is abolished, and the abomination of desolation is set up, there will be 1,290 days."

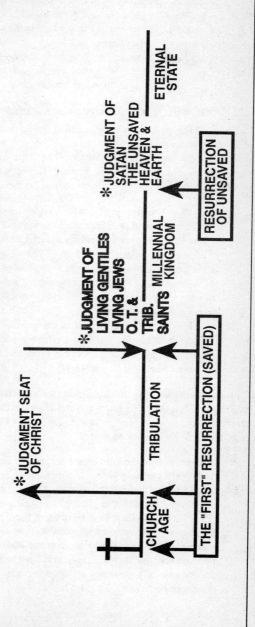

An extra 30 days are added to the normal 3½ years (1,260 days) giving a total of 1,290 days. Note that Daniel then says, "How blessed is he who keeps waiting and attains to the 1335 days" (verse 12). The extra 30 days added to the 45 days (1,335 - 45 = 1,290) comes to a total of 75 days. This will likely be the time in which the sheep and goat judgment of Matthew 25:31-46 takes place. The 75 days could also be additional time for setting up the millennium due to the devastation of the tribulation.

22. What will Jesus do after the second coming?

Jesus Christ will reign upon earth from Jerusalem for 1,000 years after His second coming. Isaiah 11:1-5 tells of the Messiah who will come from the family of David and rule the nation Israel with righteousness and absolute justice. This passage is a clear prophecy of the reign of Jesus Christ during the millennium.

> Then a shoot will spring from the stem of Jesse, and a branch from his roots will bear fruit. And the Spirit of the LORD will rest on Him, the spirit of wisdom and understanding, the spirit of counsel and strength, the spirit of knowledge and the fear of the Lord. And He will delight in the fear of the LORD, and He will not judge by what His eyes see, nor make a decision by what His ears hear; but with righteousness He will judge the poor, and decide with fairness for the afflicted of the earth; and He will strike the earth with the rod of His mouth, and with the breath of His lips He will slay the wicked. Also righteousness will be the belt about His loins, and faithfulness the belt about His waist (Isaiah 11:1-5).

Jesus Christ will be the focal point of all activity during the millennium. It will be His reign and His kingdom. That which was rejected at the time of His first coming will now be accepted and fully realized. Dr. Walvoord writes:

> In keeping with the announced purpose of God to put a man on David's throne who could rule forever, Jesus Christ will come back to assume this throne. At the present time he is in heaven awaiting this time of triumph over his enemies (Ps. 110:1-2). As the One risen from the dead (Acts 2:29-36), he is qualified to sit on the throne of God forever and without successors. His reign over the house of Israel will be from Jerusalem (Isa. 2:1-4), and from the same location he will also reign as King of Kings and Lord of Lords over the entire earth (Ps. 72:8-11,17-19).[28]

What Christ will be doing during the millennium is best understood by recognizing its characteristics. Christ's reign will be:

- *universal* (Daniel 2:35; 7:14,27; Micah 4:1,2; Zechariah 9:10)
- one of inflexible *righteousness* and *justice* (Isaiah 3:5-11; 25:2-5; 29:17-21; Micah 5:5,6,10-15; Zechariah 9:3-8)
- exercised in the *fullness of the Spirit* (Isaiah 11:2,3)
- a *unified government* (Ezekiel 37:13-28)
- *swift in dealing* with any outbreak of sin (Psalm 2:9; 72:1-4; Isaiah 11:4; 29:20,21; 65:20; 66:24; Zechariah 14:16-21; Jeremiah 31:29,30)
- An *eternal* reign (Daniel 7:14,27)

23. Is the second coming Christ's final return?

Yes, the second coming will be Christ's final return. There will not be future ascensions and returns. This seems clear in light of the fact that when Christ does return He will reign upon earth for 1,000 years (Revelation 20:1-9). After the millennium, history on earth will come to a close with the great white throne judgment (Revelation 20:11-15). At this time the current heavens and earth will be destroyed and burned up (2 Peter 3:10-12), followed by the new heavens and new earth (2 Peter 3:13; Revelation 21–22). Therefore, there will be no need for a future coming of Christ in addition to His second advent.

P A R T   5

Why Does the Second Coming Matter?

24. Why should I be concerned about the second coming?

The second coming of Jesus Christ is important for us today because it affects the priorities we set for our lives. We know what the end of human history will be and how it will unfold. Just as the prophecies of the first coming of Jesus Christ were fulfilled 2,000 years ago, so also will the prophecies of the second coming of Jesus Christ be fulfilled in the future. Dr. Carl F.H. Henry writes:

> No prophetic doctrine is more prominent in the New Testament than that of the promised personal return in great power and glory of the crucified, risen and now exalted Jesus. The certainty of Christ's second coming in the New Testament connects with the fact of his already accomplished first coming.[29]

Because of the first coming we can be certain of the second coming. Such certainty gives hope, purpose, goals, security, perspective, understanding, and meaning to even the smallest segments of daily life.

The second coming also assures us that the wrongs of this world will one day be righted. Tyranny, injustice, and deceit will come to an end in the marketplace and the great halls of power. With the righteous reign of Jesus Christ, justice will prevail.

> The last time you read of Pontius Pilate in the New Testament, two prominent Christians are begging the pagan Roman governor for the body of Jesus. The next time world rulers and kings see the body of Jesus will be on the coming judgment day when all will bow the knee to the King of kings and Lord of lords.[30]

The second coming of Christ has enormous personal, ethical, national, and international significance. It will be the greatest event of history, and its consequences will be universal and eternal.

25. How should people prepare for the second coming?

Every major Christian affirmation and creed throughout the centuries has affirmed Christ's second coming. A recognition and acceptance of this coming has been proclaimed around the world for 2,000 years.

The fact that there will be a second coming affects every person who has ever lived or will ever live. It is not a Hollywood special-effects production, religious raving, psychological paranoia, or monastery mysticism. It is a spectacular reality that will one day occur; it cannot be avoided. Regardless of what our culture proclaims or the direction in which our civilization drifts, the end of human history is in the hands of God. Dr. Henry writes of our culture and the consequences of its rejection of biblical and prophetic truth:

> The intellectual idolatries are many, all the more because they are cherished by those who have no patience with revealed religion, fixed truths, eternal commandments. The one "unthinkable" prospect for our technological society is (not the possibility of scientific destruction of modern civilization, for that prospect would congratulate the power potential of the scientific community, but rather) *divine doom!* The Second Coming of Christ, the End of all ends, the gates of hell, the resurrection of the dead, the final judgment

of mankind—these are ruled out by the wisdom of the world. . . . So there arises a herd of humanity that anesthetizes the possibilities of spiritual life and knifes itself to spiritual death, a generation with mustard-seed consciences, a society that believes in pseudo-values and pseudo-truths.[31]

The stakes of the future are very personal and very high. Either we follow the destructive dictates of culture or we follow the revealed truths of God found in the Bible. It is a high-stakes winner-take-all battle for truth, salvation, and destiny for all people.

Whoever bids earnestly for the future must bid for big stakes. The living God is history's highest bidder and, awaiting the last trump, He has already bid the incarnation, the atonement, the resurrection and a small band of redeemed fishermen.[32]

The "last trump" is the second coming of Christ. Are you ready?

Preparation for the second coming of Christ is not accomplished through insurance, survivalist techniques, stockpiling food and fuel, meditation, physical fitness, political action, fasting, or any of a multitude of other contemporary activities. Preparation for the second coming of Christ is accomplished through accepting the free offer of salvation based upon the substitutionary death of Jesus Christ for your sins.

Dr. Henry has said of contemporary society and its citizens: "The intellectual suppression of God in His revelation has precipitated the bankruptcy of a civilization that turned its back on heaven only to make its bed in hell."[33] This bold but true statement may be an accurate reflection of your own spiritual status. Is it?

Perhaps you have reached this final question in this booklet and yet do not know for sure what will be your eternal destiny. If so, then this is the most important question of the booklet for you, and we encourage you to consider carefully its contents.

We would like you to *know* that you have eternal life through Jesus Christ, God's Son. In Revelation John issues a last invitation: "And the Spirit and the bride say, 'Come.' And let the one who hears say, 'Come.' And let the one who is thirsty come; let the one who wishes take the water of life without cost" (Revelation 22:17). What does this mean?

The image is that of a wedding. The groom has issued an invitation to his bride. He is willing, but is she willing? In this same way, God has made provision for you—at no expense to you, but at great expense to Him—to enter into a relationship with Him that will give you eternal life. More specifically, the invitation is issued to the one who hears and who is thirsty. Thirst represents a need. This need is forgiveness of sin. You must recognize that you are a sinner in the eyes of God: "For all have sinned and fall short of the glory of God" (Romans 3:23). God is holy and thus cannot ignore anyone's sin. He must judge it. However, God in His mercy has provided a way by which sinful men and women can receive His forgiveness. This forgiveness was provided by Jesus Christ when He came to earth 2,000 years ago, lived a perfect life, and died on the cross in our place to pay for our sin: "For the wages of sin is death, but the free gift of God is eternal life in Christ Jesus our Lord" (Romans 6:23). The Bible also says, "Christ died for our sins according to the Scriptures, and that He was buried, and that He was raised on the third day according to the Scriptures" (1 Corinthians 15:3,4).

In order to obtain this salvation and eternal life that Jesus Christ offers, we must individually trust that Christ's payment through His death on the cross is the only way we can receive the forgiveness of our sins, the reestablishment of a relationship with God, and eternal life. "For by grace you have been saved through faith; and that not of yourselves, it is the gift of God; not as a result of works, that no one should boast" (Ephesians 2:8,9). This is why John invites the thirsty to come and enter into a relationship with God through Christ.

Are you thirsty? Do you recognize your sin before God? If you do, then come to Christ. If you don't acknowledge your need for salvation, then you bypass this opportunity. Please don't.

Those who are thirsty and want salvation can express their trust through the following prayer:

> Dear Lord, I know that I have done wrong and fallen short of Your perfect ways. I realize that my sins have separated me from You and that I deserve Your judgment. I believe that You sent Your Son, Jesus Christ, to earth to die on the cross for my sins. I put my trust in Jesus Christ and what He did on the cross as payment for my sins. Please forgive me and give me eternal life. Amen.

If you just prayed this prayer in sincerity, you are now a child of God and have eternal life. Heaven will be your eternal home. *Welcome to the family of God!* As His child you will want to develop this wonderful relationship by learning more about God through studying the Bible. You will want to find a church that teaches God's Word, encourages fellowship with other believers, and promotes the spreading of God's message of forgiveness to others.

If you were a Christian before reading this booklet, we encourage you to continue in your relationship with Christ. As you grow, you will want to live for Him in light of His coming. You will want to continue to spread the message of forgiveness you have experienced. As you see God setting the stage for the end-time drama, you should be motivated to increased service until He comes. May your heart be occupied with His words:

> Behold, I am coming quickly, and My reward is with Me, to render to every man according to what he has done. I am the Alpha and the Omega, the first and the last, the beginning and the end. Blessed are those who wash their robes, that they may have the right to the tree of life, and may enter by the gates into the city (Revelation 22:12-14).

CONCLUSION

The second coming of Jesus Christ to planet Earth is the most important future event on God's schedule. Jesus Christ and His followers will win in history—in spite of current appearances to the contrary. The second coming is the culmination of Christ conquering all His enemies, including death. He will reign victoriously for 1,000 years. This means there are solutions to the deepest problems that mankind faces, but they are found only in Jesus Christ and His Word. The current attempts to solve the world's ills using corporate solutions will never work.

Christ's return, although a future event, is to be the focus of our lives as believers. This attention should lead to great activity. His soon return is an eternal yardstick that we can use to bring proper perspective to the present. Christ's advent should motivate us to godly living, evangelism, and missionary efforts—the primary things that will bring our Lord's response of "Well done, thou good and faithful servant."

Because history is moving toward the goal of Christ's return our hearts cry out with the words of Jesus and the apostle John: "'Yes, I am coming quickly.' Amen. Come, Lord Jesus." Maranatha!

RECOMMENDED READING

Benware, Paul N. *Understanding End Times Prophecy: A Comprehensive Approach.* Chicago: Moody Press, 1995.

Blackstone, William E. *Jesus Is Coming.* New York: Revell, 1932.

Brookes, James H. *Maranatha.* New York: Fleming H. Revell Company, 1989.

Bultema, Harry. *Maranatha! A Study of Unfulfilled Prophecy.* Grand Rapids: Kregel Publications, 1985.

Campbell, Donald K. and Jeffrey L. Townsend. *A Case for Premillennialism*. Chicago: Moody Press, 1992.

Couch, Mal, ed. *Dictionary of Premillennial Theology*. Grand Rapids: Kregel Publishers, 1996.

Deere, Jack S. "Premillennialism in Revelation 20:4-6," *Bibliotheca Sacra* 135 (January–March 1978): pp. 58-73.

Feinberg, Charles L. *Millennialism: The Two Major Views,* 4th. ed. Chicago: Moody Press, 1980.

Fruchtenbaum, Arnold G. *Footsteps of the Messiah: A Study of the Sequence of Prophetic Events*. Tustin, CA: Ariel Press, 1982.

_____. *Israelology: The Missing Link in Systematic Theology*. Tustin, CA: Ariel Ministries Press, 1993.

Hindson, Ed. *Final Signs: Amazing Prophecies of the End Times*. Eugene, OR: Harvest House Publishers, 1996.

Hoyt, Herman A. *The End Times*. Chicago: Moody Press, 1969.

Ice, Thomas & Timothy Demy. *The Truth About Armageddon and the Middle East,* Pocket Prophecy series. Eugene, OR: Harvest House, 1997.

_____. *The Truth About the Rapture*, Pocket Prophecy series. Eugene, OR: Harvest House, 1996.

_____. *The Truth About Heaven and Eternity,* Pocket Prophecy series. Eugene, OR: Harvest House, 1997.

_____. *The Truth About the Millennium*, Pocket Prophecy series. Eugene, OR: Harvest House, 1996.

_____. *The Truth About Signs of the Times,* Pocket Prophecy series. Eugene, OR: Harvest House, 1997.

_____. *The Truth About 2000 A.D. and Predicting Christ's Return*, Pocket Prophecy series. Eugene, OR: Harvest House, 1996.

_____. ed. *When the Trumpet Sounds: Today's Foremost Authorities Speak Out on End-Time Controversies*. Eugene, OR: Harvest House, 1995.

LaHaye, Tim. *No Fear of the Storm: Why Christians Will Escape All the Tribulation*. Portland, OR: Multnomah Press, 1992.

Larsen, David L. *Jews, Gentiles, and the Church: A New Perspective on History and Prophecy*. Grand Rapids: Discovery House, 1995.

Lindsey, Hal. *The Rapture: Truth or Consequences*. New York: Bantam Books, 1983.

Lindsey, Hal, with C.C. Carlson. *The Late Great Planet Earth.* Grand Rapids: Zondervan, 1970.

McClain, Alva J. *The Greatness of the Kingdom: An Inductive Study of the Kingdom of God.* Winona Lake, IN: BMH Books, 1959.

Pache, René. *The Return of Jesus Christ.* Chicago: Moody Press, 1975.

Pentecost, J. Dwight. *Things to Come: A Study in Biblical Eschatology.* Grand House, 1958.

———. *Thy Kingdom Come.* Wheaton, IL: SP Publications, Inc., 1990.

Ryrie, Charles C. *The Basis of the Premillennial Faith.* Neptune, NJ: Loizeaux Brothers, 1953.

———. *Come Quickly, Lord Jesus: What You Need to Know About the Rapture.* Eugene, OR: Harvest House, 1996.

Showers, Renald. *Maranatha: Our Lord, Come!* Bellmawr, N.J.: The Friends of Israel Gospel Ministry, 1995.

Walvoord, John F. *Major Bible Prophecies: 37 Crucial Prophecies That Affect You Today.* Grand Rapids: Zondervan, 1991.

———. *The Millennial Kingdom.* Findlay, OH: Dunham Publishing Company, 1959.

———. *Armageddon, Oil and the Middle East Crisis.* Grand Rapids: Zondervan, 1990.

———. *The Church in Prophecy.* Grand Rapids: Zondervan, 1964.

———. *Israel in Prophecy.* Grand Rapids: Zondervan, 1962.

———. *The Nations in Prophecy.* Grand Rapids: Zondervan, 1967.

———. *The Return of the Lord.* Grand Rapids: Zondervan, 1955.

———. *Prophecy: 14 Essential Keys to Understanding the Final Drama.* Nashville: Thomas Nelson Publishers, 1993.

West, Nathaniel. *The Thousand Year Reign of Christ: The Classic Work on the Millennium.* Grand Rapids: Kregel Publications, 1993.

NOTES

1. Jeffrey L. Sheler, "Dark Prophecies," *U.S. News & World Report*, December 15, 1997, p. 63.

2. Walter Kaiser, *Back Toward the Future: Hints for Interpreting Biblical Prophecy* (Grand Rapids: Baker Book House, 1989), p. 20.

3. Ibid., p. 21.

4. John F. Walvoord, *Prophecy: 14 Essential Keys to Understanding the Final Drama* (Nashville: Thomas Nelson Publishers, 1993), pp. 132-33.

5. Ibid., p. 138.

6. John F. Walvoord, *Major Bible Prophecies* (Grand Rapids: Zondervan, 1991), p. 372.

7. Ibid., p. 375.

8. John F. Walvoord, *Jesus Christ Our Lord* (Grand Rapids: Zondervan, 1969), p. 279.

9. Ibid., pp. 279-80.

10. Ibid., p. 280.

11. Ibid., pp. 280-81.

12. The eight stages leading up to the second coming are adopted from Arnold Fruchtenbaum, *The Footsteps of the Messiah: A Study of the Sequence of Prophetic Events* (San Antonio: Ariel Press, 1982), pp. 216-54.

13. Walvoord, *Major Bible Prophecies*, pp. 390-91.

14. John S. Feinberg, "Arguing for the Rapture: Who Must Prove What and How" in Thomas Ice and Timothy Demy, ed., *When the Trumpet Sounds* (Eugene, OR: Harvest House Publishers, 1995), p. 194.

15. Edward E. Hindson, "The Rapture and the Return: Two Aspects of Christ's Coming" in Ice and Demy, *Trumpet Sounds*, p. 158.

16. The quotation and the first six contrasts in the the table on page 24 are taken from John F. Walvoord, *The Return of the Lord* (Grand Rapids: Zondervan, 1955), pp. 87-88.

17. Hindson, "The Rapture and the Return," p. 157.

18. Walvoord, *Return*, p. 17.

19. Many of the points in this section are taken from John F. Walvoord, *The Rapture Question,* rev. and enlarged ed. (Grand Rapids: Zondervan, 1979), pp. 274-75.

20. Charles C. Ryrie, *Revelation* (Chicago: Moody Press, 1968), pp. 35-36.

21. Walvoord, *Rapture Question,* p. 274.

22. Renald Showers, *Maranatha: Our Lord Come! A Definitive Study of the Rapture of the Church* (Bellmawr, NJ: The Friends of Israel Gospel Ministry, Inc., 1995), p. 243.

23. J. Dwight Pentecost, *Things to Come: A Study in Biblical Eschatology* (Grand Rapids: Zondervan, 1958), pp. 563-79.

24. Charles C. Ryrie, *Basic Theology* (Wheaton, IL: SP Publications, Inc., 1986), p. 511.

25. David L. Larsen, *Jews, Gentiles, and the Church* (Grand Rapids: Discovery House Publishers, 1995), p. 316.

26. Ibid., p. 317.

27. Walvoord, *Major Bible Prophecies,* p. 390.

28. Ibid.

29. Carl F.H. Henry, *Carl Henry at His Best* (Portland, OR: Multnomah Press, 1989), pp. 127-28.

30. Ibid., p. 128-29.

31. Ibid., p. 128.

32. Ibid., p. 127.

33. Carl F.H. Henry, *Twilight of a Great Civilization* (Westchester, IL: Crossway Books, 1988), p. 143.

Other Books by
Thomas Ice and Timothy J. Demy

Fast Facts on Bible Prophecy
Prophecy Watch
The Truth About A.D. 2000 and Date-Setting
The Truth About America in Bible Prophecy
The Truth About Armageddon and the Middle East
The Truth About the Antichrist and His Kingdom
The Truth About Heaven and Eternity
The Truth About Jerusalem in Bible Prophecy
The Truth About the Last Days' Temple
The Truth About the Millennium
The Truth About the Rapture
The Truth About Signs of the Times
The Truth About the Tribulation
When the Trumpet Sounds

For additional information contact:

Pre-Trib Research Center
10400 Courthouse Rd., Suite 241
Spotsylvania, VA 22553